Writing Guides

With interactive resources on CD-ROM

Realistic Stories

for ages 7–9

Sylvia Clements
and
Jillian Powell

Terms and conditions

IMPORTANT – PERMITTED USE AND WARNINGS – READ CAREFULLY BEFORE USING

Credits

Authors
Sylvia Clements and
Jillian Powell

Development Editor
Marion Archer

Editor
Sarah Sodhi

Assistant Editor
Vicky Butt

Series Designer
Anna Oliwa

Designers
Paul Stockmans and
Liz Gilbert

Cover Illustration
Mark Oliver

Illustrations
Paula Martyr and
Garry Davies

CD-ROM Development
CD-ROM developed in
association with Infuze Ltd

Designed using Adobe InDesign

Published by Scholastic Ltd,
Book End
Range Road
Witney
Oxfordshire
OX29 0YD
www.scholastic.co.uk

Printed by Bell & Bain
1 2 3 4 5 6 7 8 9   0 1 2 3 4 5 6 7 8 9

British Library Cataloguing-in-Publication Data
A catalogue record for this book is available from the British Library.
ISBN 978-1407-11263-3

Acknowledgments

The publishers gratefully acknowledge permission to reproduce the following copyright material: **Conville and Walsh** for an extract from *Why Not?* by Bel Mooney © 1991, Bel Mooney (1991, Mammoth); **David Higham Associates** for an extract from *Loudmouth Louis* by Anne Fine © 1998, Anne Fine (1998, Puffin); **David Higham Associates** for the use of an extract from *Red Eyes at Night* by Michael Morpurgo © 1998, Michael Morpurgo (1998, Hodder Children's Books); **Egmont Children's Books** for an illustration by Margaret Chamberlain from *I can't find it!* © 1985, Margaret Chamberlain (1985 Mammoth) and for use of cover illustrations by Margaret Chamberlain from *I don't want to!* by Bel Mooney © 1985, Margaret Chamberlain, *I can't find it!* by Bel Mooney © 1988 Margaret Chamberlain, *It's not fair!* by Bel Mooney © 1989, Margaret Chamberlain, *But you promised?* by Bel Mooney © 1990, Margaret Chamberlain, *Why not?* by Bel Mooney © 1990, Margaret Chamberlain and *So what!* by Bel Mooney © 2002, Margaret Chamberlain (1985; 1988; 1989; 1990; 2002 Egmont Books Ltd); **Floris Books** for an extract from *Bullies at School* by Theresa Breslin © 1993, Theresa Breslin (1993, Blackie Children's Books); **Saviour Pirotta** for an extract from 'The Fly-by-Night' by Saviour Pirotta from *Ip Dip Sky Blue* edited by Mary Hoffman © 1990 Saviour Pirotta (1990 William Collins Sons & Co Ltd); **United Agents** for an extract from *Tommy Trouble* by Stephen Potts © 2000, Stephen Potts (2000, Mammoth). Every effort has been made to trace copyright holders for the works reproduced in this book, and the publisher apologise for any inadvertent omissions.

CD-ROM Minimum specifications:

Windows 2000/XP/Vista   Mac OSX 10.4

Processor: 1 GHz	**RAM:** 512 MB	**Graphics card:** 32bit
Audio card: Yes	**CD-ROM drive speed:** 8x	**Hard disk space:** 200MB
Screen resolution: 800x600		RM CC3

Contents

Introduction: Realistic Stories

The *Writing Guides* series aims to inspire and motivate children as writers by using creative approaches. Each *Writing Guide* contains activities and photocopiable resources designed to develop children's understanding of a particular genre (for example, fairy stories). The activities are in line with the requirements of the National Curriculum and the recommendations in the *Primary Framework for Literacy*. The teacher resource books are accompanied by a CD-ROM containing a range of interactive activities and resources.

What's in the book?

The *Writing Guides* series provides a structured approach to developing children's writing. Each book is divided into four sections.

Section 1: Using good examples

Three text extracts are provided to explore the typical features of the genre.

Section 2: Developing writing

There are ten short, focussed writing tasks in this section. These are designed to develop children's ability to use the key features of the genre in their own writing. The teachers' notes explain the objective of each activity and provide guidance on delivery, including how to use the photocopiable pages and the materials on the CD-ROM.

Section 3: Writing

The three writing projects in this section require the children to produce an extended piece of writing using the key features of the genre.

Section 4: Review

This section consists of a 'Self review', 'Peer review' and 'Teacher review'. These can be used to evaluate how effectively the children have met the writing criteria for the genre.

What's on the CD-ROM?

The accompanying CD-ROM contains a range of motivating activities and resources. The activities can be used for independent work or can be used on an interactive whiteboard to enhance group teaching.

Each CD-ROM contains:

- three text extracts that illustrate the typical features of the genre
- interactive versions of selected photocopiable pages
- four photographs and an audio file to create imaginative contexts for writing
- a selection of writing templates and images which can be used to produce extended pieces of writing.

The interactive activities on the CD-ROM promote active learning and support a range of teaching approaches and learning styles. For example, drag and drop and sequencing activities will support kinaesthetic learners.

Talk for writing

Each *Writing Guide* uses the principles of 'Talk for writing' to support children's writing development by providing opportunities for them to rehearse ideas orally in preparation for writing. 'Talk for writing' is promoted using a variety of teaching strategies including discussions, questioning and drama activities (such as, developing imaginative dialogue – see *Fantasy Stories for Ages 9–11*).

How to use the CD-ROM

Start screen: click on the 'Start' button to go to the main menu.

This section contains brief instructions on how to use the CD-ROM. For more detailed guidance, go to 'How to use the CD-ROM' on the start screen or click on the 'Help' button located in the top right-hand corner of the screen.

Installing the CD-ROM

Follow the instructions on the disk to install the CD-ROM onto your computer. Once the CD-ROM is installed, navigate to the program location and double click on the program icon to open it.

Main menu screen

Main menu

The main menu provides links to all of the writing activities and resources on the CD-ROM. Clicking on a button from the main menu will take you to a sub-menu that lists all of the activities and resources in that section. From here you have the option to 'Launch' the interactive activities, which may contain more than one screen, or print out the activities for pupils to complete by hand.

If you wish to return to a previous menu, click the 'Menu' button in the top right-hand corner of the screen; this acts as a 'back' button.

Screen tools

A range of simple writing tools that can be used in all of the writing activities are contained in the toolbar at the bottom of the screen.

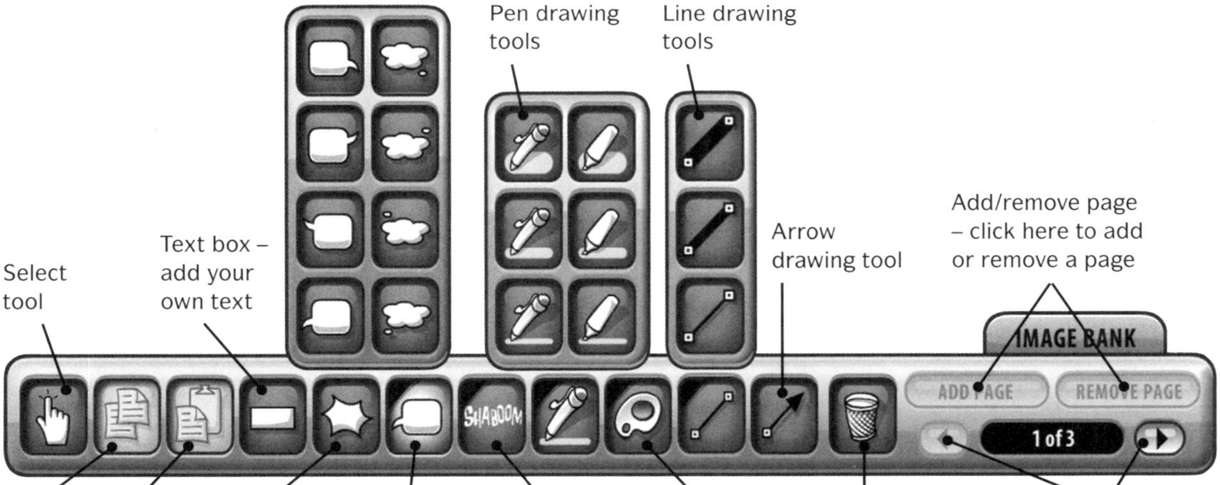

Print

Save your work to chosen files

Open – navigate to your saved file to open your previous work

Reset the page

Printing and saving work

All of the resources on the CD-ROM are printable. You can also save and retrieve any annotations made on the writing activities. Click on the 'Controls' tab on the right-hand side of the screen to access the 'Print', 'Open', 'Save' and 'Reset screen' buttons.

View all thumbnails by clicking on the arrows

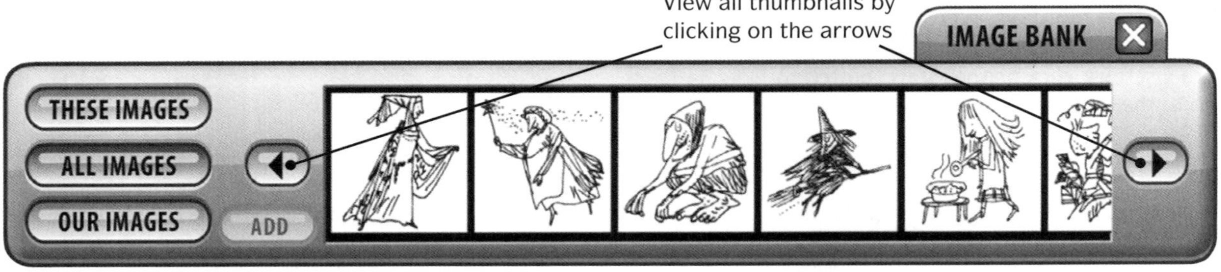

Image bank – click and drag an image to add it to an activity

Image bank

Each CD-ROM has an 'Image bank' containing images appropriate to the genre being taught. Click on the tab at the bottom right of the screen to open the 'Image bank'. On the left-hand side there are three large buttons.

- The 'These images' button will display only the images associated with the specific activity currently open.
- The 'All images' button will display all the photographs and illustrations available on the CD-ROM.
- The 'Our images' button will contain any images you or the children have added to the CD-ROM.

Press the left or right arrows to scroll through the images available. Select an image and drag and drop it into the desired location on the screen. If necessary, resize the image using the arrow icon that appears at the bottom right of the image.

You can upload images to the 'Image bank', including digital photographs or images drawn and scanned into the computer. Click on 'Our images' and then 'Add' to navigate to where the image is stored. A thumbnail picture will be added to the gallery.

Writing your own story

Each CD-ROM contains a selection of blank writing templates. The fiction genre templates will be categorised under the button 'My story' and the non-fiction templates will be categorised under 'My recount' or 'My writing'. The writing templates encourage the children to produce an extended piece of genre writing. They can also add images, speech bubbles and use other tools to enhance their work.

The fiction titles also include a cover template for the children to use. They can customise their cover by adding their own title, blurb and images.

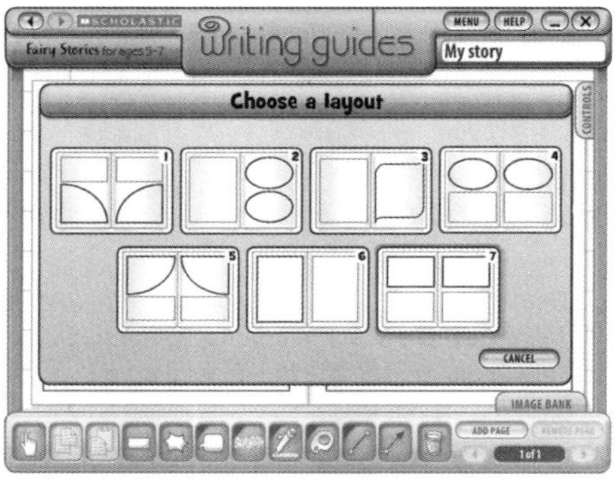

Section 1

Using good examples

Realistic stories deal with real situations, issues or dilemmas that children may experience, such as family break up, bereavement, moving house and bullying. Events are typically centred on characters within family, friendship or community groups. The story may be funny or sad or may deal with overcoming difficult situations. It may be told in the first or third person, but usually focuses on a character who is grappling with the issue, sometimes alone, and facing opposition from, or conflict with, others. Relationships are important and often the central character grows or learns in experience during the story. The reader should be able to relate to the character's feelings and actions and think 'If that were me…' or 'If I were in that situation…'. The characters should be realistic, the settings familiar and the situations probable or possible.

Through shared reading of a range of realistic stories and the extracts on the CD-ROM and photocopiable pages 10–12, children will become familiar with the key conventions of the genre and be able to draw on them for their own writing. The most fruitful writing in this genre often comes from personal experience, so you may like to suggest that the children use this as a starting point for their own ideas. Keeping a diary or holiday journal is a useful way to collect experiences and ideas to use in narrative writing.

Children will also develop their understanding of the genre by reading a wide range of titles, for example, *Bullies at School* by Theresa Breslin (Floris Books) (about bullying), *Kamla and Kate* by Jamila Gavin (Mammoth) (about friendship), *The Runner* by Keith Gray (Young Corgi) (about running away from home) and *Dolphin Boy* by Julie Bertagna (Mammoth) (about siblings, disabilities).

Links to the Primary Framework

Developing understanding of narrative texts and having opportunities to write them is an important part of literacy development in the Primary Framework for Literacy. The framework provides detailed guidance for teaching and learning about realistic stories at Key Stage 2 (stories with familiar settings; stories/short novels that raise issues). The activities in this book address objectives from all 12 strands of the Primary Framework for Literacy but with particular focus on strands 7–10.

Realistic story features

Structure
- Chronological narrative.
- Problem–conflict–climax–resolution.

Language
- First or third person narrative.
- Typically past tense.
- Dialogue reveals character and progresses action.

Characters
- Believable and sympathetic characters.

Setting
- Realistic and familiar.

Extract 1: "What's the Trouble, Tommy?"

What's on the CD-ROM

"What's the Trouble, Tommy?"
- Text extract to read and discuss.

Mind map
- Type in line numbers to highlight evidence from the extract.

This extract from *Tommy Trouble* by Stephen Potts features a boy facing sadness and difficulties in his home and school life. It demonstrates how emotive language can help us understand and empathise with a character's feelings. Tommy has an absent father, is failing at his schoolwork and is ridiculed by his teacher and classmates.

- Open the extract on the CD-ROM. Read it with the children, going over any difficult vocabulary ('droned', 'paralysed', 'winced') as necessary.
- Ask: *How is Tommy feeling and why?* Come up with some descriptive words with the children, such as 'sad', 'upset' and 'distracted'. Ask the children what the lesson is about and what Tommy is actually thinking about (missing his father).
- Ask the children to pick out words that convey Tommy's discomfort ('stiffened', 'winced') and circle or underline them. Focus on the teacher's character and ask the children to highlight descriptive words, including a metaphor that creates a sense of menace ('prowled'; 'the creeping shadow of a growling cloud').
- Open 'Mind map' from the CD-ROM. Explain to the children that they need to find evidence of each statement in the extract and fill in the boxes using the line numbers found on photocopiable page 10. Alternatively, they can do this activity using photocopiable page 13.

Extract 2: Explain!

What's on the CD-ROM

Explain!
- Text extract to read and discuss.

Whose words?
- Drag and drop the dialogue to the correct speech bubbles.

Why not? by Bel Mooney is a story about a child's rebellion against what she sees as over-protective parenting. The extract shows how dialogue can be used to convey a character's feelings and progress the plot.

- Open the extract 'Explain!' on the CD-ROM and read it with the children. Ask: *What does Kitty argue about with her mum?* Ask the children to briefly explain what Kitty and her Mum feel and why. (Kitty feels confident to walk to school on her own; her mum thinks she is still too young and is worried that something bad will happen to her.)
- Discuss what the children think Mum's reasons are and why she might not want to explain them to Kitty. Is it just because she feels she doesn't have to or is there more to it? (She may not want to worry or frighten Kitty about what could happen to her.)
- Hand out photocopiable page 14 'Between the lines' and ask the children to complete it in pairs.
- Open 'Whose words?' from the CD-ROM. Invite the children to drag the dialogue to the correct speech bubbles and then on paper write some reasons each character might give for the way they feel. Alternatively, they can complete photocopiable page 15.

Extract 3: Runaway

What's on the CD-ROM

Runaway
- Text extract to read, discuss and edit.

Right choice!
- Click on the correct answers to multiple-choice questions.

In this extract, Jem has run away from home and has to find a place to sleep rough. The emphasis is on descriptive writing and how it can be used to create an atmospheric setting and reflect a character's mood or feelings.

- Open the extract 'Runaway' on the CD-ROM and read it with the children, circling and exploring any difficult vocabulary ('lurid', 'sentries', 'predatory') as necessary.
- Ask the children to explain what they think has happened to Jem and speculate on why. (He is sleeping rough because he has run away from home because he is unhappy or bad things have been happening to him there.)
- Examine the descriptive writing together. Ask: *What sights and sounds help to evoke the atmosphere?* Can the children identify adjectives, adverbs, examples of similes ('stood like sentries') and metaphors ('the flash of an urban fox')? Circle or underline these as they find them.
- Open 'Right choice!' from the CD-ROM. Work through the questions as a shared activity. Alternatively, let them complete photocopiable page 16.
- When they have finished, consider how the descriptive language conveys Jem's surroundings as well as how he is feeling (cold, uncomfortable and a bit scared).

Poster: Get real!

What's on the CD-ROM

Get real!
- Roll over the thought bubbles to reveal prompt questions.

This poster displays question prompts to help children plan or analyse realistic stories. Children can refer back to the poster to analyse key features when reading examples of the genre and use it to help them develop ideas when writing their own realistic stories.

- Display 'Get real!' from the CD-ROM. Roll over the thought bubbles and work through the questions as they appear on the screen.
- Hand out photocopiable page 18 'Get real!' and explain to the children that they can refer back to this poster when they need to check their own realistic stories or assess other examples of the genre.
- When the children are familiar with the poster, hand out photocopiable page 17 'Resolution'. Explain that the children are going to re-read all three extracts from pages 10–12 and fill in each section, deciding what they think might happen in the plot and how the story might end.
- Encourage volunteers to share their ideas on how the stories might develop and decide as a class which ideas work best and why.

Extract 1: "What's the Trouble, Tommy?"

Mr Sutherland's voice droned on at the front of the class, while Tommy gazed out of the window near the back. There wasn't much to see. He turned back to the classroom, looking over the rows of desks in front of him to the blackboard, where the squiggles made no more sense than usual. Tommy knew he should concentrate, but he couldn't. He stared at the long line of marks on the top of his jotter – one for each day his dad had been gone – and sadly added another.

"Remembrance Day began after the First World War." Mr Sutherland squiggled on the blackboard as he spoke. "They called it the war to end all wars, but twenty-one years later there was another one, even bigger. The Second World War. On Sunday we remember both of them. This is one of the most famous poems from the first – the Great War. I'd like you to copy it into your jotters."

Tommy grasped his pencil tight, his tongue between his teeth, and set to work as the teacher prowled about. Bent ever closer over his book, he felt Mr Sutherland approach from behind, the creeping shadow of a growling cloud.

"What's all this, Thomas Cameron?" Mr Sutherland asked, sliding the jotter off the desk. Tommy's paralysed pencil left a thick grey line on the page, like a smoke trail from a plane about to crash. Tommy stiffened: whenever a teacher used his full name, it spelt trouble. Mr Sutherland read from the board:

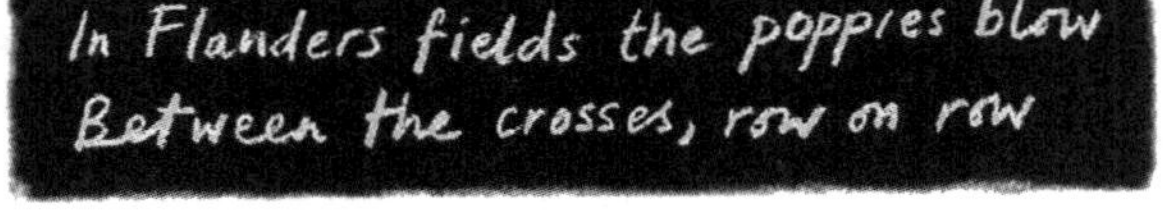

And then from Tommy's jotter:

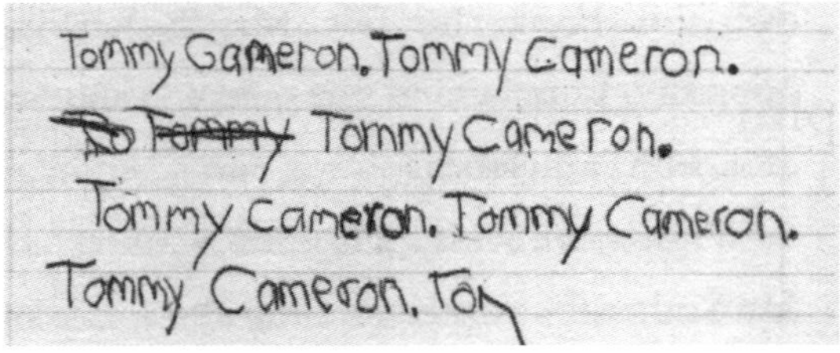

Tommy winced. Nearby classmates nudged each other into titters.

Mr Sutherland flicked back through the pages to yesterday's lesson, and beyond. "Tommy Cameron. Tommy Cameron. Tommy Cameron," he read again.

He put the jotter down with a sigh. Tommy stared hard at the desk top. "What's the trouble, Tommy? Can't write? Can't read? Or just can't be bothered?"

From *Tommy Trouble* by Stephen Potts

Extract 2: Explain!

Kitty always used to say she didn't want to do this or that. Then there was a change – *she* wanted to do things, but the grown-ups wouldn't let her. Instead of saying, "I don't want to!" she found herself asking, "Why not?" Very often.

One day, for example, she asked Mum if she could walk to school on her own. "No," said Mum firmly.

"Why not?"

"You know why not," smiled Mum.

"No, I don't!"

Mum thought. "Well, because you might have an accident."

"But there's a lollipop lady!"

"Anyway, you're too young."

"Lots of my friends go to school on their own. So why not me?"

"Because." Mum wasn't smiling now.

"Because what?" asked Kitty.

"Because I said so," said Mum, folding her arms.

"That's not a good reason," said Kitty.

When she went to school she told William and Rosie what had happened. "Oh, my mum always says that," sighed Rosie.

"So does mine," said William.

"It's not fair," said Kitty. "Grown-ups never think they have to explain things."

"They wouldn't like it if we acted the same," said Rosie.

Just then, the bell went – but Kitty had started to think. And at play-time she told William and Rosie her plan.

"Do you both think we should be allowed to go to school on our own, instead of being treated like babies?"

"Yes," said Rosie and William.

"And do you think grown-ups should give proper *reasons*?" Kitty asked.

They agreed.

"Well here's what we do…" said Kitty.

From *Why not?* by Bel Mooney

Extract 3: Runaway

Jem dragged the cardboard box into the alleyway. He saw the flash of an urban fox as tin cans clattered across the rain-streaked pavement. Above, a neon light cast a lurid glare. Car headlights arched yellow beams over a row of rubbish bins that stood like sentries, offering protection. Behind them, he would be hidden from the traffic and predatory passers-by.

As boxes went, it was a good one. The picture on the side showed that it had once contained a shiny new household appliance. Now, the box was more precious to Jem than any gadget. He searched inside for anything that might be useful. A piece of tape – that might help tie down the bin bag that he hoped would protect him from the rain. He pulled the sleeping bag from the straps of his rucksack and pushed it into the box. These were his worldly goods now: a box, a sleeping bag and a broken umbrella scrounged from a skip.

Jem shuffled his body inside the box, feeling the cold hardness of the concrete beneath him. He pulled the bin bag around the box and tried to wedge the umbrella over his head, but the wind kept catching underneath it, threatening to whisk it away. How on earth was he going to sleep like this?

Mind map

- We can tell a lot about Tommy from this extract. The mind map below shows what we know.
- Find evidence in the extract to support these statements. Write the line number in the box to show where you found the evidence.

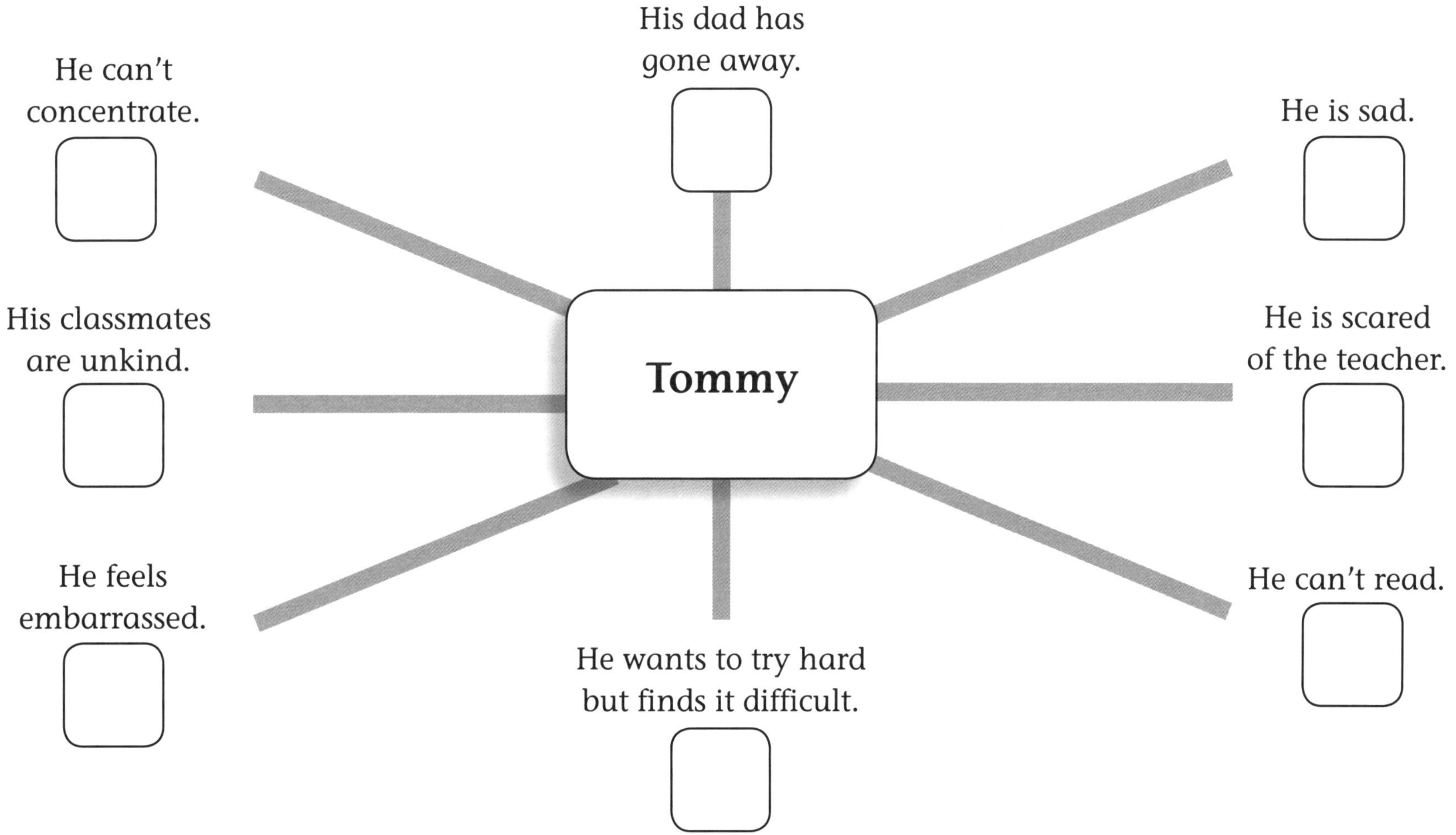

Between the lines

- Write down some evidence from 'Explain!' to support each of the following statements. Decide if the evidence is dialogue or description.

Statement	Dialogue	Description
Kitty is behaving differently as she gets older.		
Mum is not going to change her mind.		
Mum is losing patience.		
Kitty doesn't understand mum's reasons.		
Kitty uses facts to support her argument.		
The argument with Mum gives Kitty an idea.		
Kitty seeks help from her friends.		

Whose words?

• Kitty has just asked to walk to school on her own. Decide which words are Mum's and which are Kitty's. Write the correct name in each speech bubble and add a number to show in what order they are said.

"Why not?"

______________ ☐

"No."

______________ ☐

"But there's a lollipop lady!"

______________ ☐

"Lots of my friends go to school on their own. So why not me?"

______________ ☐

"You might have an accident."

______________ ☐

"Anyway, you're too young."

______________ ☐

"That's not a good reason."

______________ ☐

"Because I said so."

______________ ☐

Right choice!

- Tick two correct answers for each question.

1 In the story, Jem is sleeping rough:

in a city ☐ in the country ☐
in a main street ☐ in a backstreet ☐

2 Jem sees lights from:

a neon sign ☐ shop windows ☐
car headlights ☐ a torch ☐

3 The weather is:

sunny ☐ snowy ☐ windy ☐ rainy ☐

4 Jem wants to get away from:

sentries ☐ predatory passers-by ☐ a fox ☐ the traffic ☐

5 Jem is feeling:

cold ☐ angry ☐ uncomfortable ☐ sorry ☐

6 Jem finds and keeps:

a sleeping bag ☐ some tape ☐
a broken umbrella ☐ a rucksack ☐

7 Jem uses the bin bag:

to cover the box ☐ to carry his things ☐
to keep the rain off ☐ to sleep in ☐

Resolution

- Realistic stories have a clear structure. The three extracts introduce a problem or dilemma that the main character has to overcome.
- Can you decide what happens and how each story ends?

"What's the Trouble, Tommy?"

The problem: ______________________________

The cause of the problem: ______________________________

The climax: ______________________________

The resolution: ______________________________

Explain!

The problem: ______________________________

The cause of the problem: ______________________________

The climax: ______________________________

The resolution: ______________________________

Runaway

The problem: ______________________________

The cause of the problem: ______________________________

The climax: ______________________________

The resolution: ______________________________

Get real!

- What is the theme of the story?
- What issue or problem does the main character face?
- Where does the story take place?
- Who is the main character?
- What is the main character like?
- What helps the main character to resolve the problem?
- How is the problem resolved?

Illustration © 1985, Margaret Chamberlain.

Section 2

Developing writing

The activities in this section prompt children to expand and develop their ideas about issues they might like to write about, develop a main character, create supporting characters, decide on and create a realistic setting, and develop convincing dialogue. The children will draw on their experience of the genre gained from the extracts in Section 1, their own reading and their own experiences of different real-life issues.

The activities provide scaffolded support for developing plot, character and setting. They also generate ideas and vocabulary for realistic stories, and encourage children to develop an appropriate writing style, making use of description, dialogue and action.

Plot

There are opportunities to explore different pathways for plotlines using trigger ideas.

Setting

Children are given opportunities to choose and develop different realistic settings for their stories and to explore how descriptions of settings can help to convey a character's feelings and predicament.

Character

Children focus on developing key characters through description and dialogue and use drama and role play to improvise and develop dialogue.

How to use the activities

Each activity is accompanied by detailed teachers' notes giving guidance on delivery, including how to use the photocopiable pages at the end of the section and the materials on the CD-ROM. Children are encouraged to experiment with a variety of forms. There is strong emphasis on class or group discussion and role play throughout this section. This will help children get to the heart of issues they are exploring and to empathise with their characters, as well as developing speaking and listening skills. The activities can be adapted to suit different class situations. They should be modelled for the whole class or smaller groups, before children are asked to undertake independent work.

Activity breakdown

Activity 1: Issues

Objective

To sustain conversation, explain or give reasons for their views or choices. (Year 3 Strand 1)

What to do

In this lesson, children explore issues for realistic plotlines by relating them to their own experiences.

- Work with the children in small groups and hand out sets of cards cut from photocopiable page 25 'Issues'. Explain that these represent more stories by Bel Mooney, the author of the extract 'Explain!' (on photocopiable page 11).
- Ask the groups to shuffle the cards and then discuss examples from their own experiences that relate to each title. For example, 'It's not fair!' might relate to how they feel about a sibling getting all the attention at home, or getting away with things when they don't.
- Allow them time to shuffle the pack of cards and discuss two or more issues.
- Bring the class back together and invite volunteers from the groups to relate experiences that illustrate each of the issues. Record their suggestions on the board, under the title headings.

Activity 2: What's the problem?

Objective

To use some drama strategies to explore stories or issues. (Year 3 Strand 4)

What to do

This activity uses role play to explore issues as starting points for stories.

- Work with the children in small groups and give each group one of the scenario cards from photocopiable page 26 'What's the problem?'.
- Ask each group to develop a short role play based around the issue shown on their card. Encourage them to think about the characters that are involved in their scenario, how they are feeling and how they might demonstrate their feelings (through what they say, the tone of their voice, their expressions and so on).
- Once the groups have developed their scenes, gather the class together to watch the groups take turns to perform. Can the children guess what the issue was?
- Encourage the children to begin to collect an ideas bank of issues/ dilemmas. They can source them from other stories they read, from other media (newspapers or news reports on television) and from their own experiences.

Activity 3: Story openings

Objective

To identify and make notes of the main points of section(s) of text.
(Year 3 Strand 7)

What to do

This activity encourages children to think about opening paragraphs and how to introduce the issue and characters of a story.

- Provide the children with different opening paragraphs cut out from photocopiable page 27 'Story openings'. Ask volunteers to read them aloud. Discuss what we find out, how the author introduces the main issue of the story (such as bullying or a new school) and who the main character is.
- Find the trigger points that initiate action in the scene (for example, in *Bullies at School*, it is the shouted insult). For each extract, prompt the children to identify the style of writing (such as description, direct speech, a confession) and whether the stories are written in the first or third person. Record their answers in table form on the board under these headings: title of story; issue; trigger point; style; narrative.
- Discuss some possible pathways for the story to follow, encouraging the children to explore different ideas for each. For example, might the storyline be humorous or might it be hard-hitting and emotional?
- As an extension activity, encourage the children to explore the opening paragraphs of more stories, such as *Kamla and Kate* by Jamila Gavin (Mammoth) or *The Diddakoi* by Rumer Godden (Macmillan). Encourage them to use the same headers to create their own tables.

Activity 4: Work it out!

Objective

To develop and refine ideas in writing using planning and problem-solving strategies.
(Year 4 Strand 9)

What's on the CD-ROM

Work it out!

- Type in answers to questions to form a story plan.

What to do

In this activity, children choose one of the story scenarios from photocopiable page 26 'What's the problem?' and develop the idea using a scaffolded planner.

- Recap some of the story scenarios from Activity 2, using the prompt cards from photocopiable page 26 'What's the problem?'.
- Ask the children to choose one of the ideas to develop into the outline of a realistic story. Explain that they first need to decide on a main character, a supporting character or confidant (this could be a person, a pet or even a toy), and someone with whom there is a conflict.
- Open 'Work it out!' from the CD-ROM and work through the questions, typing in the children's suggested answers. Reflect on whether the story is going to be humorous and light-hearted, or more hard-hitting and serious. Alternatively, the children could complete this activity on individual whiteboards or using photocopiable page 28.
- As an extension activity, ask the children to use the table template from Activity 3 to consolidate their ideas for the story, deciding on a title, issue, trigger point, style and narrative form.

Activity 5: Create a character

Objective

To use settings and characterisation to engage readers' interest.
(Year 4 Strand 9)

What's on the CD-ROM

Create a character
- Type in features to create a character.

What to do

This activity focuses on developing the main character for a realistic story.

- Tell the children they are going to develop the main character for the story they planned in Activity 4.
- First, discuss the characters who feature in the three extracts from Section 1. Re-read the extracts together, inviting the children to pick out any salient information about the characters – whether they are a boy or girl, how old they are, what we learn about their home/family life, and what characteristics they display. Briefly discuss what a main character needs to be (believable, likeable, someone we want to succeed) and why (so we are engaged in reading about them).
- Open 'Create a character' from the CD-ROM. Consider each feature in turn, typing the children's suggestions in the boxes. Alternatively, invite them to do this activity using photocopiable page 29.
- Encourage the children to go on to develop their own ideas for a character to feature in any of the story scenarios from Activity 2 using photocopiable page 29.

Activity 6: Settings

Objective

To use settings and characterisation to engage readers' interest.
(Year 4 Strand 9)

What's on the CD-ROM

Settings
- Click on the cards to select a setting.

What to do

This activity focuses on describing a setting for a realistic story.

- Open 'Settings' from the CD-ROM or distribute photocopiable page 30. Explain to the children that they are going to pick a setting for the events that happen in a realistic story, then develop it by thinking about the details of description, the events that take place and how the main character feels when he or she is there.
- In the first set of three cards click on one card to reveal a general setting, and then click on one card from the second set to choose the exact location in the setting.
- Hand out photocopiable page 31 'Describe a setting'. With the children working in pairs, tell them to work together to develop the setting by completing each section.
- In a further session, let the children work on computers to pick another setting before filling in the photocopiable sheets again to develop their ideas for a realistic story.

Activity 7: What's going on?

Objective

To present events and characters through dialogue to engage the interest of an audience. (Year 3 Strand 4)

What's on the CD-ROM

Media resources

- Listen to, discuss and use the audio clip as a stimulus for plots.

What to do

In this activity, children use role play to develop a story idea from an audio clip.

- Listen to the audio clip in the 'Media resources' section of the CD-ROM. Discuss the kind of scenario it conjures up in the children's imaginations (a visitor, someone with good news, someone with bad news, someone in trouble). Ask: *What sort of mood does it conjure up?* (Something exciting, worrying, unexpected?)
- Suggest that arrivals, whether a visitor, letter, parcel, email or text message, work well as trigger points in realistic stories as they can initiate action and change.
- Ask the children to work in pairs to think up a scenario using the audio clip as the hook. Invite them to improvise a short scene that explains what is going on. Allow them time to plan and improvise their scenes.
- Bring the class back together and ask pairs to perform their scenes for the class. Invite constructive feedback, discussing which ideas seem most fruitful and why.

Activity 8: Plot pathways

Objective

To use the language of possibility to investigate and reflect on feelings, behaviour or relationships. (Year 3 Strand 3)

What's on the CD-ROM

Media resources

- Use the four images as stimulus for writing.

What to do

In this activity, children use images as prompts to discuss atmosphere and develop different plot pathways.

- Open the 'Media resources' section on the CD-ROM and click on an image. Ask the children to describe what they see and speculate on what is going on and what sort of mood or feelings the image suggests.
- Write these headings on the board: event; feelings; what led up to it; what happens next? Briefly explain what they cover: What is happening in the scene? How does/do the character(s) involved feel? What events have led up to the scene? What might happen next?
- Encourage the children to explore different pathways (for example, the child packing the suitcase might be preparing to go on holiday or running away from home). Discuss different ideas and record the best suggestions under the headings.
- Repeat the exercise by clicking on a second image, again recording the children's suggestions under the same headings on the board and considering different pathways, humorous or serious.
- Allow the children to view all four images and in pairs select one image to plan plot pathways using the headings.
- Invite them to go on to develop one of the pathways using photocopiable page 28 'Work it out'.

Activity 9: How does it feel?

Objective

To use the language of possibility to investigate and reflect on feelings, behaviour or relationships. (Year 3 Strand 3)

What's on the CD-ROM

How does it feel?

- Drag and drop the feelings to match the correct extract.

What to do

This lesson encourages children to think how to develop characters by exploring and conveying their feelings.

- Explain to the children that a character's feelings will change through the story as the issue progresses to a resolution. For example, they might be feeling frightened and unhappy at the outset if they are confronting bullies, but during the story they may find a way of fighting back, and so by the end they may have found a new confidence and self-belief.
- Open 'How does it feel?' from the CD-ROM or distribute photocopiable page 32. Read through the extracts together and invite volunteers to drag and drop the feeling they think fits each of them. Encourage the children to give their reasons verbally.
- Highlight different parts of speech (verbs, adjectives, adverbs) that suggest the feeling, and identify the style (direct speech or description).
- As an extension activity, encourage the children to try writing their own sentences to convey each feeling.

Activity 10: Talk, talk

Objective

To present events and characters through dialogue to engage the interest of an audience. (Year 3 Strand 4)

What's on the CD-ROM

Talk, talk

- Roll over speech bubbles to reveal children's quotes.
- Type in dialogue.

What to do

This activity focuses on writing dialogue.

- Open 'Talk, talk' from the CD-ROM and roll over one of the speech bubbles to reveal a child's quote. Invite the children to suggest dialogue that might be spoken between the characters involved. Encourage them to rehearse their ideas orally before you type them in.
- Repeat the exercise by rolling over another speech bubble. Alternatively, let the children complete the activity on photocopiable page 33.
- Hand out photocopiable page 34 'Direct speech' and tell the children to work in pairs to complete it by developing one piece of dialogue from the activity 'Talk, talk'.
- You may want to model an example of dialogue with description before they begin. For example, Daniel's speech bubble could be developed as follows: *"Get out of the way, Danny! I want to use the computer." Daniel's brother elbowed his way to the computer. "But it's my turn. Tell him Dad!" Daniel argued.*

Issues

- Cut out each card and discuss how these issues relate to your own experiences.

What's the problem?

- Read the following cards and decide what the problem is. Act out a short drama based on one idea.

It wasn't fair. Why did Mum always believe my brother?

"Why can't I have a pet? All my friends do." I argued.

"If you do that," I told Tilly, "you're not my friend any more."

That morning, Dad had his first quarrel with our new neighbours.

"But I don't want to choose between you and Dad," I cried.

Being the new boy at my school is not much fun.

Story openings

Red Eyes at Night

By Michael Morpurgo

My cousin Geraldine is a real little toad. Every summer holidays it's the same – Geraldine comes to stay. And who has to look after her?

I do, because there's no-one else.

Loudmouth Louis

By Anne Fine

It was my own fault, I admit.

I could have been in the group that chose to organise the Raffle. But I was too busy chatting to bother to put up my hand.

And I could have joined the group Miss Sparkes said could run the Bring-And-Buy Stall. But I was leaning across to whisper something to George, so I missed that chance too.

Bullies at School

By Theresa Breslin

"SPECKY-WECKY FOUR-EYES! WECKY-SPECKY FOUR EYES!"

Siobhan Cunningham hitched her school rucksack further up her back and started to move more slowly along the road. She could now see the group at the school gate who were doing all the shouting, Karen Williams and her friends, Lyn, Rosie, Benny and Peter. They usually hung about there every morning, waiting for someone to pick on, and the someone was usually her.

The Fly-by-Night

By Saviour Pirotta

When Biddy Beck was eight, she and her mum moved from the country to a flat in a large town. Biddy liked her new home, high up in a tower block. She loved her bedroom with its green carpet, and she liked to look down on the conker trees below.

The only thing Biddy didn't like in the new town was her new school. It was huge and dark. There was a high wall round the playground. Worst of all, the children in it looked tough and unfriendly.

Work it out!

- Write down your chosen issue or theme in the star box.
- Answer the questions to record ideas for the structure of your story.

① Where and how will the story start?

② Who has the problem?

③ Who else is involved?

Issue

⑥ How might the issue be resolved?

④ Who could the character talk to or go to for help?

⑤ How will the issue develop?

Create a character

- Develop your main character, writing their features in the following boxes.

Name:

Family:

Appearance:

Best friend/confidant(e):

Likes:

Dislikes:

Settings

- Choose one of these settings for your story.

Home ☐

School ☐

Away ☐

- Choose from three options for your exact setting.

Kitchen ☐

Classroom ☐

City ☐

Living room ☐

Playground ☐

Countryside ☐

Garden ☐

School hall ☐

Seaside ☐

Describe a setting

- Think about your chosen setting and answer the questions below.

What is this place like?

Describe an event in your story that happens here.

What does your character like about the place?

What does your character dislike about the place?

Which three things about this place will you describe in detail?

1. ______________________

2. ______________________

3. ______________________

How does it feel?

- Draw lines to match the feelings to the correct extract.

Laura bounced across the room. Her face was beaming.	A tear rolled down his cheek as he saw the empty cage.	It's not fair. My little sister gets all the attention.

sad **afraid** **happy**

upset **jealous** **angry**

"Don't you dare talk to me like that!" Mum thundered.	John's mouth had gone dry. His heart was racing as he opened the front door.	"I can't bear it!" I cried. "You can't make me choose, I can't do it!"

Talk, talk

- Read the quotes, then in the speech bubbles, add dialogue to suggest what the characters might say to each other.

"My big brother bosses me around."
Daniel, aged 8

Daniel | Daniel's brother

"I don't know if I want my mum to have another baby."
Kerry, aged 7

Kerry | Kerry's friend

"I was sad when my dog died."
Rashid, aged 8

Rashid | Rashid's friend

"I get bullied because I am tall."
Caitlin, aged 9

Caitlin | A bully

Direct speech

- Use your work on the 'Talk, talk' sheet to develop one conversation.

Character 1

Character 2

Feeling

Feeling

1.

2.

- On another sheet of paper write this as a piece of dialogue with description. Don't forget to use speech marks!

Section 3

Writing

Once they have read a range of realistic stories and extracts, explored key features of the genre and completed the activities in Sections 1 and 2, the children will be ready to attempt an extended piece of writing. The three writing projects in this section provide opportunities for them to develop and write an original realistic story. The timescale for completing the three writing projects can be flexible. In order to progress from initial ideas to finished stories, the children will need a number of extended writing sessions.

Practising skills

The three extended writing projects outlined in this section all provide opportunities for children to develop their speaking, listening and writing skills.

- For oral work, children can discuss as a class, in small groups or with a writing partner.
- For shared writing, they will learn how to use a planning frame to plan a realistic story then turn the ideas in a shared story plan into written text using the 'My realistic story' writing templates on the CD-ROM.
- For independent work, they can use the writing frames to plan and write their own realistic stories. They can present these on screen using the 'My realistic story' writing templates on the CD-ROM or on paper as a piece of extended writing.

The first project provides a starter idea for the children to develop into a plotline. The second project challenges the children to sequence images to tell a story then use the storyboard to draft and flesh out the plotline. In the third project, the children can choose a theme and supporting characters to feature in their story, then use the story planner and writing templates to construct and develop the plot.

Providing support

Provide feedback and support for the children as they plan and write their own stories. Encourage them to consider how they can edit and improve their plans using prompts from the poster 'Get real!' on photocopiable page 18 or by referring to the interactive version of the poster on the CD-ROM. Refer back to activities completed in previous sessions so that children can draw on their knowledge of realistic stories read in class.

Writing tips

When writing a realistic story:

- Write in the first or third person and past tense.
- Create a likeable main character.
- Draw on your own personal experiences where possible.
- Present your character with an issue or problem to resolve.
- Use dialogue to convey characters' feelings.
- Structure the story with an opening, a problem or issue that reaches a climax, and a resolution at the end.

Project 1: Story starter

Objective

To develop and refine ideas in writing using planning and problem-solving strategies. (Year 4 Strand 9)

What's on the CD-ROM

Story starter
- Type in answers to questions.

Story planner
- Complete the plan.

My realistic story
- Compose a story.

What to do

This project allows children to plan and write an original realistic story using a structured planner.

- Open 'Story starter' from the CD-ROM or distribute photocopiable page 38. Discuss then type in possible answers to each question to generate ideas for a new story.
- Display 'Story planner' on the CD-ROM and, as a class, answer the questions to develop the story plan.
- Open 'My realistic story' from the CD-ROM. Using the shared story plan, begin drafting a simple story. Model how to use the writing templates. Involve the children at all stages of the writing process.
- Once the children are clear about the process encourage them to independently produce a detailed plan using either photocopiable page 42 'Story planner' or by navigating to the CD-ROM activity.
- Before they begin composing their own story using the writing templates, provide the children with photocopiable page 18 'Get real!' and photocopiable page 43 'Write with style'. They can refer back to these for planning and writing tips. Ask them to plan, draft and write their story working from the story plans.

Project 2: Storyboard

Objective

To use beginning, middle and end to write narratives in which events are sequenced logically and conflicts resolved. (Year 3 Strand 9)

What's on the CD-ROM

Picture story
- Drag and drop images into a story sequence.

Story planner
- Complete the plan.

My realistic story
- Compose a story.

What to do

In this project, children work out how to sequence images to tell a story, then use a storyboard to develop and flesh out the plotline.

- Open 'Picture story' from the CD-ROM or distribute photocopiable page 39. Look at the images together and discuss how to sequence them to tell a realistic story. Encourage the children to give their reasons, using visual clues (for example, the boy sees the headmaster after the test results).
- Invite volunteers to drag and drop (or cut and stick) the images into the right order. Encourage others to rehearse the outline of the story orally, correcting the order if necessary.
- Distribute photocopiable page 40 'Storyboard'. Explain that a storyboard is often used by filmmakers to plan the action of a story, scene by scene, when they are filming. Tell the children to fill in each scene, referring back to the sequence of images in 'Picture story' and recording the characters who feature, the setting, what happens (the action) and how they think the main character is feeling.
- The children should then produce a more detailed plan by navigating to the 'Story planner' on the CD-ROM or using photocopiable page 42. They can then compose their story using the writing templates.

Project 3: Pick and mix

Objective

To develop and refine ideas in writing using planning and problem-solving strategies. (Year 4 Strand 9)

What's on the CD-ROM

Pick and mix
- Pick a theme for a realistic story.
- Pick two supporting characters to feature in the story.
- Type in story ideas.

Story planner
- Complete the plan.

My realistic story
- Compose a story.

What to do

This project offers children different choices to trigger ideas for a realistic story.

- Open 'Pick and mix' from the CD-ROM. Click on a theme and invite the children to suggest ideas for how to develop it.
- Next, click on two supporting characters. Challenge the children to think how the characters might feature in a story about the chosen theme.
- Explain to the children that they are going to plan and write a story choosing one of the themes and picking two characters to feature in the story.
- Click on more cards to explore different combinations. Encourage the children to explore the possibilities; for example, a troublemaker might feature in a story about bullying, or a toy companion in a story about a family problem.
- Using the theme and two characters selected by the class type in notes to plan a realistic story.
- Alternatively, copy and cut out a set of themes and characters from photocopiable page 41 'Pick and mix' and hold up each card for the children to consider and make their choices.
- Provide the children with time to plan and write their own realistic stories, using the 'Story planner' and 'My realistic story' writing templates from the CD-ROM.

Story starter

- Imagine a letter, email or text arrives that will change the life of your main character. Build on this idea by answering the questions below.

What does the letter, email or text say?

Who is it from?

How will it change your character's life?

How does he or she feel about it?

What does he or she do?

How are things resolved in the end?

Picture story

- Look at the six images, then cut and paste them in the right order to tell a story.

Storyboard

- Describe what is happening in each scene of 'Picture story'. Record details of characters, setting, action and feelings.

❶ Characters:

Setting:

Action:

Feelings:

❷ Characters:

Setting:

Action:

Feelings:

❸ Characters:

Setting:

Action:

Feelings:

❹ Characters:

Setting:

Action:

Feelings:

❺ Characters:

Setting:

Action:

Feelings:

❻ Characters:

Setting:

Action:

Feelings:

Pick and mix

- Choose a theme for your realistic story.

A false friend	A family problem
Bullying	Something lost

- Choose two supporting characters for your realistic story.

A toy or animal companion	A good friend
An unhelpful neighbour	A troublemaker

Story planner

- Use these prompts to help you plan your realistic story. Write your notes below.

What is the title of your story? ______________________

What issue or problem is your story about? ______________________

____

Will you write in the first (I) or third (he/she) person? ______________________

Who is your main character? ______________________

____

Who are your supporting characters? ______________________

____

Where is your story set? ______________________

____

What details of setting will you include? ______________________

____

How will you start your story? ______________________

____

What will the climax of your story be? ______________________

____

How will your story end? ______________________

____

Write with style

Use effective speech words:
sighed, muttered, shouted, mumbled, explained.

Use a mixture of long and short sentences for effect and turn sentences into exclamations:
Amy gasped!
The rain beat steadily on the window. Amy gazed outside. She felt as gloomy as the weather.

When your character is thinking, use questions to illustrate his or her thoughts:
"Will I ever be happy again?" wondered Amy sadly to herself.

Use dialogue effectively, incorporating action to show how the character is feeling:
"I'm not going!" Amy shouted, stamping her foot and slamming her bag on the floor. "It's just not fair!" She burst into tears and collapsed in a heap on the bed.

Use adjectives and adverbs – but don't overuse!
Amy turned and sadly waved goodbye. She dragged her heavy school bag along the floor as she slowly made her way home.

Use time phrases to progress the story – but be realistic:
It wasn't long before…
Soon, the time had come to…
The following morning…
After what seemed like hours…

Review

The activities in this section encourage children to look critically at their own work and will also help them to evaluate any realistic stories they read. It provides you with an opportunity to review the children's progress in achieving specific learning targets and to assess their overall attainment at the end of the unit against national standards.

In assessing the children's realistic writing, it may be necessary to counterbalance a tendency to take stories into the realms of adventure or fantasy. The children should understand that when writing in this genre, characters, setting and plot all need to stay rooted in the familiar and everyday. They should be encouraged to keep a diary or journal to record personal experiences which they can draw on as a resource in their realistic writing. Writing notes or taking photographs of places that could provide interesting backdrops can help to provide detail to bring story settings alive.

Self review

Involve children as much as possible in the assessment process. Photocopiable page 45 'Self review' is a self-assessment tool that can be used by the children independently to review how successful they have been in using some of the characteristic styles or language features of the realistic genre in their own writing. They can use the review sheets provided here as a checklist, then practise skills in editing and improving their draft instructions. You may wish to model the self review process first, using one of the shared stories created by the class.

Peer review

Photocopiable page 46 'Peer review' encourages the use of review partners to help the children review and edit their written work. Organise the children to work with a partner of similar ability. Tell them to read and then review their partner's realistic story by answering the questions on the photocopiable sheet. Provide opportunities for feedback. Remind them that their comments should be constructive and supportive.

Teacher review

The grid on photocopiable page 47 'Teacher review' has been designed to enable you to assess children's progress and attainment in writing at the end of a unit of work on realistic stories. It is linked to the National Curriculum's eight Assessment Focuses for writing. It is important to include observation of speaking and listening skills as well as assessment of written work. Carrying out a review will enable you to evaluate the progress that children have made towards achieving specific learning goals. The findings of the review should be used to set individual and group learning targets and to ensure that the next steps in learning for all children are planned at the appropriate level. The review may also highlight gaps, which can be addressed by revisiting relevant sections.

Self review

- Read your realistic story and review it by completing the sections below.

I think I did these things well:

I think I could have improved these things:

Feature bank

use of time phrases	creating a main character	use of trigger points
use of chapters	using objects to help the action	description of setting
use of exclamations	creating an exciting climax	use of dialogue
use of questions	creating a satisfying resolution	introduction of the problem

This is the main change I would make to improve my story:

Illustration © 2003, Paula Martyr.

Peer review

- Read your partner's realistic story and review it by completing the sections below.

Story title: ______________________________

Author: ______________________________

1. Is the issue the main character faces clear?	Yes/No
2. Do you feel as if you know and understand the main character?	Yes/No
3. Is there a conflict in the story?	Yes/No
4. Does the story have a setting that you can imagine?	Yes/No
5. Does the author use dialogue to help the storyline?	Yes/No
6. Does the story have an exciting climax?	Yes/No
7. Were you happy with the resolutions to the story?	Yes/No

If you have answered **No** to any of the above questions, give suggestions for how you would improve this area of the story:

List three things which you thought were good about this story (parts of the plot/effective adjectives or adverbs/trigger points):

1. ______________________________

2. ______________________________

3. ______________________________

Teacher review

	AF5 Vary sentences for clarity, purpose and effect.	**AF6** Write with technical accuracy of syntax and punctuation in phrases, clauses and sentences.	**AF3** Organise and present whole texts effectively, sequencing and structuring information, ideas and events.	**AF4** Construct paragraphs and use cohesion within and between paragraphs.	**AF1** Write imaginative, interesting and thoughtful texts.	**AF2** Produce texts which are appropriate to task, reader and purpose.	**AF7** Select appropriate and effective vocabulary.
LEVEL 3	Some complex sentences using subordinating connectives (*e.g. if, because*). Some limited variation in tense and verb forms.	Punctuation to demarcate sentences usually accurate. Some use of speech punctuation. Commas used to divide clauses in narrative.	Openings and closings usually signalled. Attempt to sequence narrative logically.	Some links between sentences within paragraphs (*e.g. using pronouns*).	Ideas and content appropriate to realistic genre included (*e.g. realistic settings, believable characters*). Attempt to adopt narrative viewpoint (first or third person).	Some attempts at style appropriate to realistic genre (*e.g. familiar/ everyday*).	Simple vocabulary, generally appropriate for realistic genre used (*e.g. language rooted in the familiar/ everyday*). Some words selected for effect or occasion (*e.g. punchy dialogue*).
LEVEL 4	Some variety in length, structure or subject of sentences. Use of some subordinating connectives (*e.g. if, when, because*). Some variation in tense and verb forms (*e.g. past tense, participles*).	Sentences demarcated accurately throughout the text. Speech marks to denote speech with some other speech punctuation (*e.g. question marks, exclamation marks*). Commas used to mark clauses.	Narrative organised by time sequence.	Paragraphs help to organise narrative content.	Ideas and content relevant to realistic story chosen. Narrative viewpoint established and maintained (first or third person).	Main features of realistic form are clear and appropriate (*e.g. familiar setting, believable characters*). Style generally appropriate to realistic genre (*e.g. rooted in the familiar/everyday*).	Some evidence of deliberate vocabulary choices (*e.g. synonyms for 'said'*).

SCHOLASTIC

Also available in this series:

ISBN 978-1407-11253-4

ISBN 978-1407-11265-7

ISBN 978-1407-11267-1

ISBN 978-1407-11256-5

ISBN 978-1407-11270-1

ISBN 978-1407-11248-0

ISBN 978-1407-11254-1

ISBN 978-1407-11266-4

ISBN 978-1407-11258-9

ISBN 978-1407-11268-8

ISBN 978-1407-11251-0

ISBN 978-1407-11257-2

ISBN 978-1407-11255-8

ISBN 978-1407-11269-5

ISBN 978-1407-11250-3

ISBN 978-1407-11247-3

ISBN 978-1407-11252-7

ISBN 978-1407-11264-0

ISBN 978-1407-11249-7

ISBN 978-1407-11260-2

ISBN 978-1407-11261-9

ISBN 978-1407-11263-3

ISBN 978-1407-11259-6

ISBN 978-1407-11262-6

To find out more, call: **0845 603 9091** or visit our website: **www.scholastic.co.uk**